Hurricane Katrina

By Sean Callery

Free digital book

Read incredible and heartwarming stories of the brave people who lived through Hurricane Katrina in your free digital book.

Katrina

survivor stories

A digital companion to **Hurricane Katrina**

SCHOLASTIC disc

Download your all-new digital book,

Katrina Survivor Stories

Log on to
www.scholastic.com/discovermore

Enter this special code:

RCHKFXD779W3

2

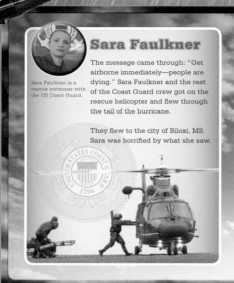

Sara Faulkner

Sara Faulkner is a rescue swimmer with the US Coast Guard.

The message came through: "Get airborne immediately—people are dying." Sara Faulkner and the rest of the Coast Guard crew got on the rescue helicopter and flew through the tail of the hurricane.

They flew to the city of Biloxi, MS. Sara was horrified by what she saw.

You could see where winds had ripped the buildings completely apart. You saw buildings pulled out to sea.

A rescue swimmer is lowered from a helicopter in a hoist.

Mayday The helicopter's radio picked up a weak Mayday signal, an emergency cry for help. An old woman and her two daughters were trapped on a boat. The old woman was very sick. She had been in the water for hours. Sara lifted her up into the helicopter and they quickly flew to the hospital.

This was the first of 52 rescues Sara made over two days.

Continued . . .

Read amazing true stories, like how one Coast Guard rescue swimmer saved 52 people who were trapped in their homes.

There are activities and quizzes to help you find out more about hurricanes.

What would you take?

If you had to leave your home in a hurry, what would you take with you? Click on the pictures below to see what might be a good idea—and what wouldn't.

GROCERIES

CRACKERS

FRESH FRESH FRESH

FIRST AID

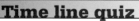

Time line quiz

Follow Hurricane Katrina as it forms and travels across the Gulf Coast. Answer the questions as you go.

Where did Hurricane Katrina start?	When did Katrina hit Florida?	How much of New Orleans was underwater?	How deep was the flooding in New Orleans?
(A) Pacific Ocean	(A) April 25, 2005	(A) 80 percent	(A) 2 feet (0.6 m)
(B) Indian Ocean	(B) August 25, 2005	(B) 50 percent	(B) 12 feet (3.6 m)
(C) Atlantic Ocean	(C) December 25, 2005	(C) 10 percent	(C) 20 feet (6 m)

It's simple to get your digital book. Go to the website (see left), enter the code, and download the book. Make sure you open it using Adobe Reader.

more

Literacy Consultant:
Barbara Russ,
21st Century Community
Learning Center Director for
Winooski (Vermont) School District

Library of Congress Cataloging-in-Publication
Data Available

ISBN 978-0-545-82956-4

10 9 8 7 6 5 4 3 2 1   15 16 17 18 19

Printed in Singapore   46
First edition, June 2015

Contents

Storm coming

Storm coming

"I know the powers that be say not to panic. I'm telling you: Panic, worry, run. The birds are gone. Get out of town! Now! Don't stay! Leave! Save yourself while you can. Go . . . go . . . go."
—Garland Robinette, New Orleans radio announcer, on Sunday, August 28, 2005

Destroyer

Hurricane Katrina was a 350-mile-wide (563 km) monster that took 1,836 lives and cost billions of dollars. It whirled through cities, towns, and farmland, blowing lives apart.

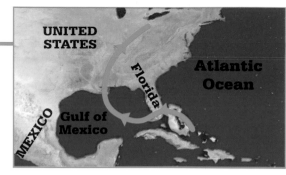

Katrina's path

Katrina started over the Atlantic. It hit Florida, then spun into the Gulf of Mexico and the Gulf Coast.

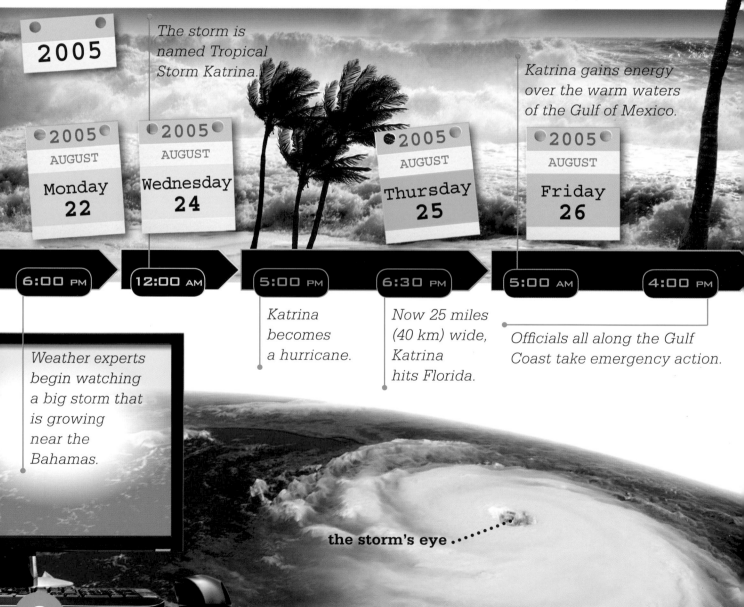

2005

The storm is named Tropical Storm Katrina.

Katrina gains energy over the warm waters of the Gulf of Mexico.

2005
AUGUST
Monday
22

2005
AUGUST
Wednesday
24

2005
AUGUST
Thursday
25

2005
AUGUST
Friday
26

6:00 PM | 12:00 AM | 5:00 PM | 6:30 PM | 5:00 AM | 4:00 PM

Weather experts begin watching a big storm that is growing near the Bahamas.

Katrina becomes a hurricane.

Now 25 miles (40 km) wide, Katrina hits Florida.

Officials all along the Gulf Coast take emergency action.

the storm's eye ....

By nightfall on August 28, 1.2 million people (80 percent

URGENT — WEATHER MESSAGE
NATIONAL WEATHER SERVICE NEW ORLEANS LA
1011 AM CDT SUN AUG 28 2005

DEVASTATING DAMAGE EXPECTED...
HURRICANE KATRINA...A MOST POWERFUL
HURRICANE WITH UNPRECEDENTED STRENGTH...
RIVALING THE INTENSITY OF HURRICANE
CAMILLE OF 1969. MOST OF THE AREA WILL BE
UNINHABITABLE FOR WEEKS...PERHAPS LONGER.
AT LEAST ONE-HALF OF WELL-CONSTRUCTED
HOMES WILL HAVE ROOF AND WALL FAILURE.
ALL GABLED ROOFS WILL FAIL...LEAVING THOSE
HOMES SEVERELY DAMAGED OR DESTROYED.

Emergency
The National Weather Service sent out its strongest warning ever about the dangers of a coming storm.

Everyone in New Orleans is told to leave (mandatory evacuation).

About 112,000 people do not have cars.

2005
AUGUST
Saturday 27

2005
AUGUST
Sunday 28

11:41 AM

1:00 PM

7:00 AM

10:00 AM

12:00 PM

Louisiana governor Kathleen Blanco telephones President George W. Bush, who declares a federal state of emergency.

New Orleans mayor Ray Nagin declares a citywide state of emergency.

The National Hurricane Center warns that Katrina is now a Category 5 hurricane.

EVACUATION ROUTE

The Superdome, the city's sports stadium, opens as a shelter for those who cannot leave.

of the population) had left the New Orleans area.

The birth of Katrina

Katrina began on August 22 as a storm out at sea. Over five days, it grew into one of the most dangerous Category 5 hurricanes ever to strike the United States.

What is a hurricane?

Hurricanes are the world's most violent storms. They form over warm seas. Winds suck up moisture and form thunderclouds. The winds usually move west and can cause serious damage.

HURRICANE FACT ATTACK

EYE WALL

The strongest winds form in the eye wall, a ring of thunderstorms in the hurricane's center.

HURRICANE SEASON

Every year, on average, six Atlantic thunderstorms grow into hurricanes. There were four Category 5 hurricanes in 2005—the most ever in a single year.

STORM SURGE

A hurricane can cause an unusual rise in sea level called a storm surge.

Katrina was a highly destructive hurricane because it

The Saffir-Simpson scale measures the strength of a hurricane.

 74–95 mph (119–153 kph)
Some wind damage and flooding

 96–110 mph (154–177 kph)
Damage to houses, small trees torn up

 111–129 mph (178–208 kph)
Major damage to roads and trees

 130–156 mph (209–251 kph)
Roofs lift off, large trees uprooted

 157+ mph (252+ kph)
Buildings collapse, major flooding

The eye is a calm area at the storm's center, inside the eye wall.

Getting faster

Hurricane Katrina blew in from the Atlantic, crossing the Gulf of Mexico on its way toward land. Its fastest wind speed was 175 mph (282 kph).

developed two eye walls.

Hurricane hunters

Weather experts watched Katrina from space, from the sea, and even from inside the storm itself.

Into the storm
Hurricane hunters flew planes right into Katrina ten times. They were measuring the storm's strength.

Tracking the storm

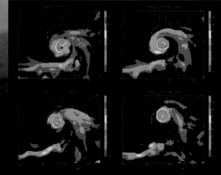

Satellites
Satellites watched Katrina from space, tracking its changes in size and direction.

Weather stations
Stations on the ground collected data on air pressure, wind strength, rainfall, and more.

Data buoys
These floating weather stations measured the giant waves that the hurricane created.

Planes dropped 153 dropsondes into Katrina to watch

" Flying into a hurricane can be turbulent at times. You feel like you're on a roller coaster—for ten hours. "

—**Shirley Murillo, NOAA research meteorologist**

Weather boats

Ships provided local weather stations with details about the conditions at sea.

Dropsondes

These small measuring devices were dropped from airplanes into the eye of the hurricane. They sent back data twice a second.

the storm from the inside.

The Gulf Coast

This beautiful and important part of the United States is home to cities including New Orleans, Gulfport, and Biloxi.

Natural defenses

Hurricanes are part of life on the Gulf Coast. Barrier islands slow down storm surges heading for land. And when a hurricane hits, nearby wetlands soak up some of the floodwaters like sponges.

Oil!
Nearly 4,000 oil rigs in the gulf provide more than 90 percent of the United States' oil and gas.

Big catch
Fishing is a big industry. The gulf provides 80 percent of the country's shrimp catch.

Shipping
Ships loaded with huge containers go into and out of New Orleans and Gulfport.

More than 150 rivers flow into

NEW ORLEANS, LA

PASCAGOULA, MS

BILOXI, MS

CHANDELEUR ISLANDS

GULFPORT, MS

GULF OF MEXICO

BURAS-TRIUMPH, LA (landfall)

Find out more about what happened on the Gulf Coast on pages 48–49.

New Orleans
The city of New Orleans is an amazing melting pot of culture, food, and music.

Beaches
Tourists love the many great beaches that stretch along the Gulf Coast.

Wetlands
These are home to many wild animals, including alligators and pelicans.

the Gulf of Mexico.

New Orleans

The city of New Orleans has always been under threat from storms and flooding. Levees (barriers) were built to keep the water out.

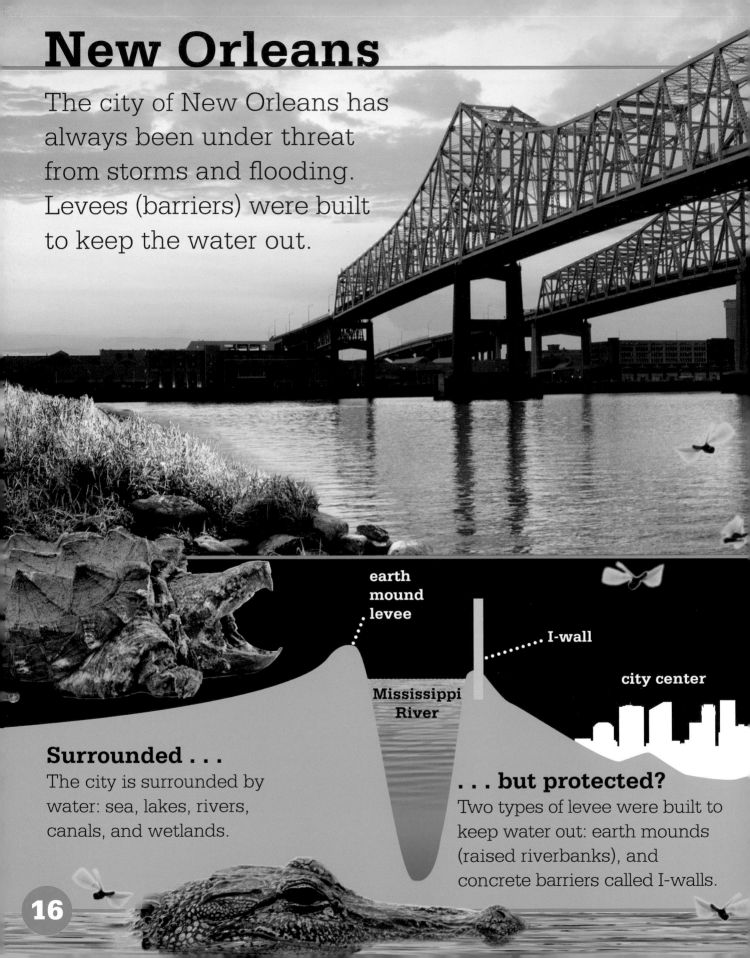

earth mound levee

I-wall

Mississippi River

city center

Surrounded . . .

The city is surrounded by water: sea, lakes, rivers, canals, and wetlands.

. . . but protected?

Two types of levee were built to keep water out: earth mounds (raised riverbanks), and concrete barriers called I-walls.

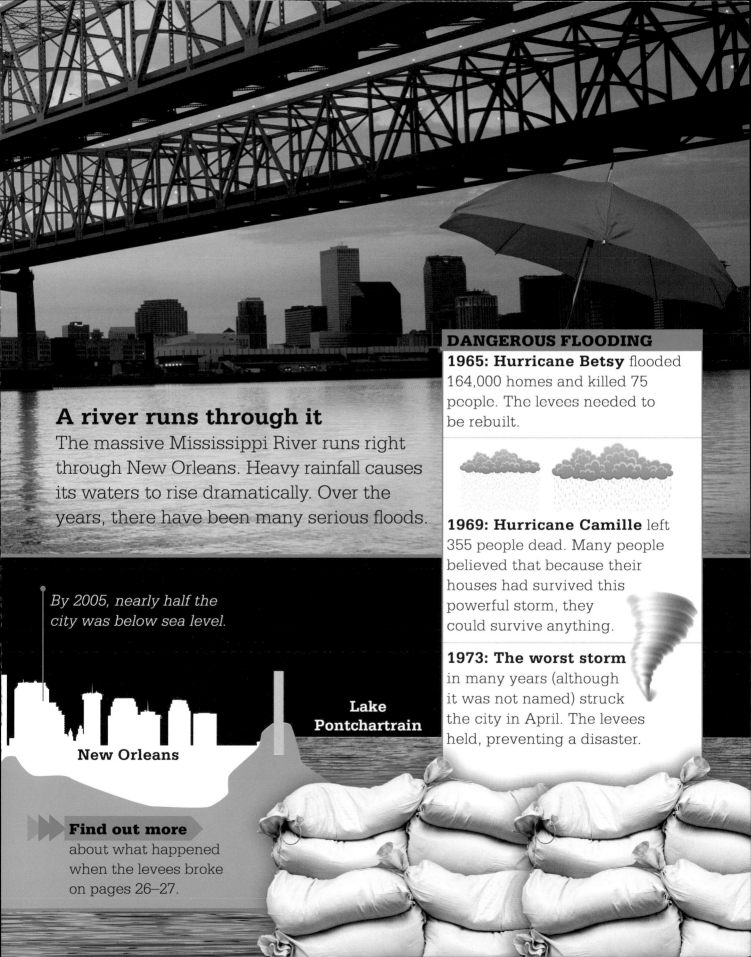

A river runs through it

The massive Mississippi River runs right through New Orleans. Heavy rainfall causes its waters to rise dramatically. Over the years, there have been many serious floods.

By 2005, nearly half the city was below sea level.

New Orleans

Lake Pontchartrain

▶▶ **Find out more** ▶
about what happened
when the levees broke
on pages 26–27.

DANGEROUS FLOODING

1965: Hurricane Betsy flooded 164,000 homes and killed 75 people. The levees needed to be rebuilt.

1969: Hurricane Camille left 355 people dead. Many people believed that because their houses had survived this powerful storm, they could survive anything.

1973: The worst storm in many years (although it was not named) struck the city in April. The levees held, preventing a disaster.

Stay or go?

2005
AUGUST
Saturday
27

2005
AUGUST
Sunday
28

By Saturday morning, it was clear that Katrina was heading directly for New Orleans. There wasn't much time. . . .

Staying in the city

Those who were staying in New Orleans needed to stock up on food, water, fuel, and batteries. Many had done this before when other hurricanes threatened.

Shelter

The Superdome opened as the largest of ten shelters for people who could not leave. By Sunday evening, 10,000 people had arrived at the Superdome with their belongings.

> " It was the scariest road trip I'd ever taken. . . . [It] was like watching some Hollywood disaster movie, only worse, because I was in it. "
>
> —Laurel Smith, Slidell, LA

Getting out!

By mid-morning on Sunday, Katrina had grown into a Category 5 hurricane. At 10:00 AM, Mayor Ray Nagin said that everyone had to leave New Orleans. It was no longer safe to stay. People piled into cars, taking as much as they could with them.

Evacuation

Cars carrying 1.2 million people streamed out of New Orleans. All those people thought they would be able to return only a few days later.

Use all exits

Officials opened up both sides of major roads to help drivers leave. But the traffic was so heavy that even short journeys to safety took many hours.

Landfall

"I heard [my husband] screaming. 'Get up here, get up here!' . . . Within seconds, the house started swaying back and forth. We both just stood there watching in total disbelief at what was happening to our home. The fierce wind was pounding our house to death, and the water was rising quickly."
—Elizabeth Ashe Havrilla, New Orleans

The storm in New Orleans

Early on the morning of August 29, shrieking winds gusting at up to 125 mph (201 kph) tore whole buildings apart. Waves up to 27 feet (8 m) high turned streets into rivers, washing away cars and homes.

Heavy rain, swept in by high winds, falls all night.

Katrina strikes land at Buras-Triumph, LA.

The powerful center of the storm smashes 30-foot (9 m) waves into Biloxi and Gulfport, MS.

Governor Blanco calls the president to ask for help.

● **2005**
AUGUST
Sunday 28

● **2005**
AUGUST
Monday 29

| OVERNIGHT | 6:10 AM | 6:30 AM | 7:30 AM | 9:45 AM | 11:00 AM | 8:00 PM |

By morning, the wetlands surrounding New Orleans cannot hold any more water.

Levees protecting eastern New Orleans fail, and water pours into the city.

Parts of the Industrial Canal wall break up. The Ninth Ward, a district of New Orleans, starts to flood.

More levees break, sending water flowing into much of New Orleans, including midtown.

Katrina wrecked 90,000 square miles (233,000 sq km)

Monday evening

New Orleans was full of destroyed buildings and was without electricity, gas, water, or phones.

> 66 We witnessed firsthand the destruction of our home and loss of every single possession we owned. 99
>
> —**Elizabeth Ashe Havrilla, New Orleans**

2005 AUGUST Tuesday 30

About 60,000 people are trapped in New Orleans, many in attics or on roofs.

2005 AUGUST Wednesday 31

A curfew is imposed in New Orleans to ensure safety, ordering people to stay off the streets until 8:00 the next morning.

Katrina fades away in northern Quebec.

2005 SEPTEMBER Thursday 1

60,000

6:00 AM

12:00 PM

6:00 PM

11:00 PM

Water is still flowing in through the many gaps in the New Orleans levees.

Water stops flowing from Lake Pontchartrain into New Orleans. The water level settles. Most of the city is flooded.

flooded streets

The head of homeland security in New Orleans, Terry Ebbert, calls the situation there "a national emergency."

across Louisiana, Mississippi, and Alabama.

The levees fail

The canals and levees of New Orleans could not handle the massive storm surge's 27-foot-high (8 m) waves. The levees cracked and broke, and water crashed into the city.

● 2005 ●
AUGUST
Monday
29

The flood begins . . .

New Orleans had flooded before. People expected to survive this storm, too. But the streets and alleyways began to fill with water.

. . . and goes on . . .

The water kept rising. Many people were forced up, into their attics or onto roofs. Others waded through the waters, heading for higher ground.

Water from Lake Pontchartrain flowed into the

Breached!

Tall waves poured over the tops of some levees. Others were weakened as water soaked into the ground underneath, or by the huge weight of water pressing on them.

. . . for days!

Some streets disappeared under 20 feet (6 m) of water. People clung to anything that could keep them afloat and alive.

city for two days.

Destruction

The winds and water wrecked many homes.

> 66 Thousands of people . . . became homeless overnight. The only possessions they had left were the clothes on their backs and in their bags. 99

—**Irwin Thompson,**
Dallas Morning News

27

Water everywhere

Katrina was one of the worst natural disasters in US history. No one was prepared for the amount of damage.

13.6 in. (35 cm) of rain fell in 24 hours over parts of New Orleans

70% of homes along the Mississippi Gulf Coast were wrecked

169 miles (272 km) of levees in New Orleans were damaged

60,000 people were stranded in their homes, often in attics or on roofs

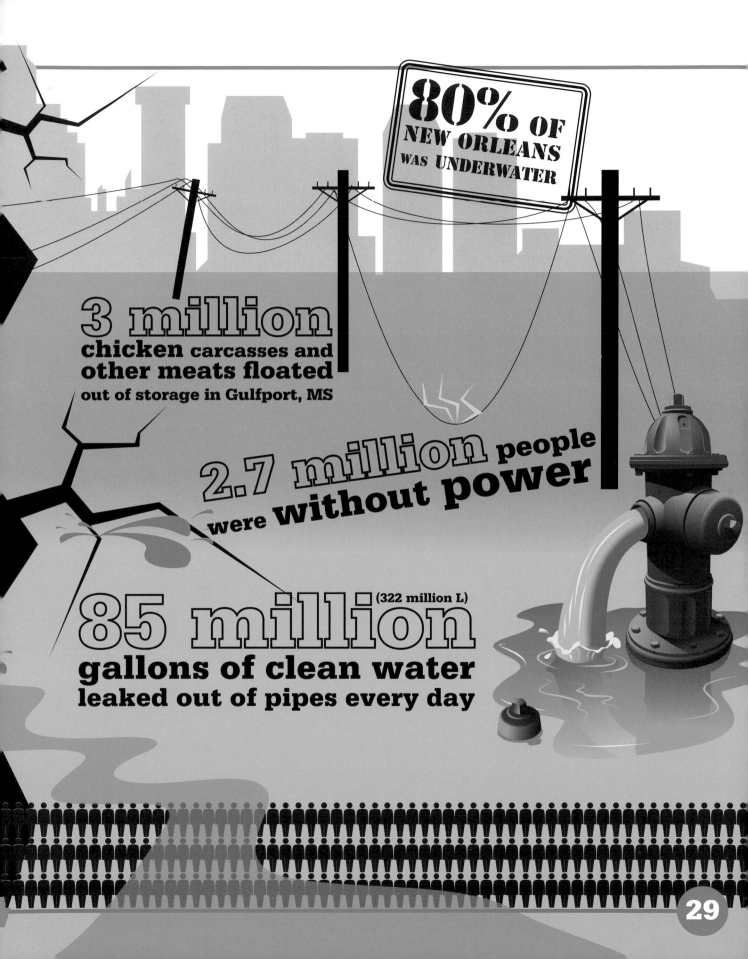

80% OF NEW ORLEANS WAS UNDERWATER

3 million chicken carcasses and other meats floated out of storage in Gulfport, MS

2.7 million people were without power

85 million (322 million L) gallons of clean water leaked out of pipes every day

Flooded city

2005
AUGUST
Tuesday 30

Water filled the streets and buildings of New Orleans to a depth of 20 feet (6 m).

30

The Ninth Ward was the neighborhood that got the

Find out more about the dangers in New Orleans on pages 40–41.

Big trouble

Only 8 of the city's 73 neighborhoods stayed dry. Because of the flooding, there was no power or fresh water anywhere in the city.

worst of the storm.

Evacuees

People whose homes were destroyed or flooded headed for dry ground and shelter. They were able to take only what they could carry, so many had no spare clothes.

Superdome
The Superdome became home to around 25,000 people. But food and water began to run out.

Convention Center
The Morial Convention Center became crowded with thousands of families who had lost their homes.

Stranded
People waited on small areas above the floodwaters to be rescued by boat or helicopter.

There was no safe running water, and bottled water soon became difficult to find.

EYEWITNESS Leaving the city

> 66 Day Two: . . . I'm woken by this horrible sound. Bits of the roof are blowing off. I sit terrified, curled up on a plastic seat. No one tells us what is happening. 99
>
> **—ReeRee Rockette, British tourist, in the Superdome**

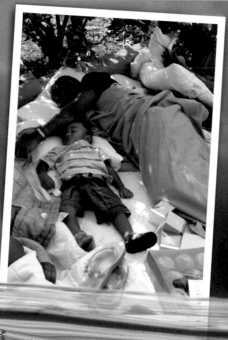

On the road
Buses dropped off evacuees on the roads that led out of the city. Many camped out there.

No shelter
Some people simply found dry ground and claimed a spot.

Evacuation
Buses carried people to safety along the Gulf Coast and to shelters in other states.

Search and rescue

Coast Guard helicopter

Coast Guard

The US Coast Guard rescued about 33,000 people. They lowered swimmers to help people escape.

There were still thousands of people trapped in their homes. They could be reached only by boat or helicopter.

Help!

Communications systems were down all over the city. Search and rescue teams, including members of the US Army and Coast Guard as well as police and other emergency workers, looked for signs of life.

Helicopters flew   **day and night,**

Other rescue agencies

FEMA
The Federal Emergency Management Agency was in charge of organizing the rescue teams.

US Navy
Ships launched search and rescue helicopters and supplied water and other goods.

Firefighters
Firefighters from all over the country volunteered to find and rescue people.

Local knowledge
Many residents of New Orleans found boats and went from house to house, listening for the cries and knocks of people who needed saving.

using night-vision equipment in the darkness.

Heroes

There were many acts of heroism after Katrina struck. Here are just a few stories.

CAPTAIN RICKY McCURLEY
This local firefighter led a team of 30 into eastern New Orleans to help 18,000–19,000 people evacuate. McCurley's team was ordered out but refused to leave because people there still needed help.

KENNY BELLAU
A professional cyclist, Bellau returned to his hometown of New Orleans, found a boat, and saved more than 400 trapped people.

JOHN KELLER
Ex-Marine Keller looked after 244 people, many of them old or disabled. He swam to get food and medicine, then organized their safe evacuation.

Jane Garrison of the Humane Society helped rescue

SARA FAULKNER

Faulkner, a rescue swimmer with the Coast Guard, saved 52 people, including small children and babies.

JIM OSBORNE

This mail carrier from Florida put together a ten-boat convoy with others from the South Florida Airboat Association. They saved more than 175 people.

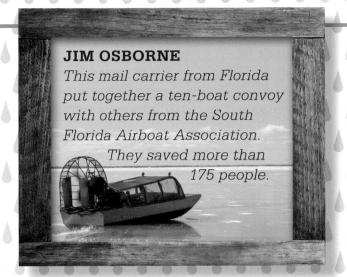

DR. NORMAN McSWAIN

The chief of trauma surgery at Charity Hospital waded through the floodwaters to get help.

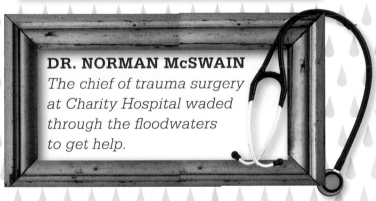

DEAMONTE LOVE

Rescuers found seven children wandering near an evacuation point in central New Orleans. The oldest, Deamonte Love, was only six years old, but he was carrying a baby and leading the other five children. They were all holding hands. A helicopter had rescued them without their parents. Their families later found them.

KATRINA THE DOG

Renamed after the hurricane, this brave Labrador retriever helped a drowning man to higher ground before being rescued herself.

thousands of animals.

Damage

Katrina wrecked 70 miles (113 km) of the Gulf Coast, blasting water far inland. An area of 90,000 square miles (233,000 sq km) was devastated.

No way out, no help in

Bridges
Bridges, including the 2-mile-long (3 km) St. Louis Bay Bridge, collapsed like dominoes.

Trains
All the train tracks along the coast were blocked by thousands of fallen trees.

Roads
Highways were covered in debris, slowing rescue services.

Cast ashore
Many fishing boats were stranded on land.

Hundreds of heavy steel shipping containers were

All gone!
Houses and other buildings were "slabbed"—only the flat concrete bases were left. Everything else was blown or washed away.

Returning home
People were shocked when they saw the damage.

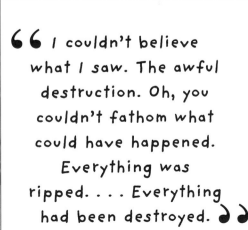

> 66 I couldn't believe what I saw. The awful destruction. Oh, you couldn't fathom what could have happened. Everything was ripped. . . . Everything had been destroyed. 99
>
> —Father Louis Lohan, Long Beach, MS

pushed 0.3 miles (0.5 km) inland.

Danger!

Parts of New Orleans and the Gulf Coast were completely destroyed by the storm. There were dangers everywhere.

The water carried raw waste from the broken sewage system.

Dangerous depths The water was murky with

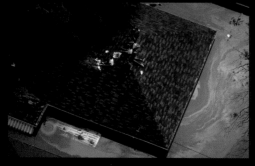

Drowning
Water rose inside buildings and threatened to drown those who could not escape.

Dirt and disease
It carried oil from flooded cars, and rotting food from burst fridges and freezers.

Nearly 200 alligators escaped from one alligator ranch

FIRE!

Thousands of broken gas lines meant that a spark could set escaping gas alight. Many people used candles for light, which created another fire hazard.

MORE DANGERS

NO POWER
There was no power or street lighting, and phones didn't work.

NO FOOD
Hungry, thirsty people raided shops.

NO LAW
With police officers busy with search and rescue, at times it was difficult to keep order.

dirt and other hazards.

Many feared there were alligators lurking in the depths.

Deadly beasts
There were animals in the water, including venomous snakes.

when it flooded.

Aftermath

"My wife and I . . . felt this calling to come to New Orleans, not just to be part of the resurgence of the football team, . . . but to be a part of the rebirth of this city."
—Drew Brees, New Orleans Saints quarterback

Recovery

Katrina made the Gulf Coast look like a war zone. It has taken years to recover from the damage that the storm caused.

Cleaning up
It wasn't only houses that were destroyed—at the airport, winds overturned planes.

2005 SEPTEMBER Friday 2

2005 SEPTEMBER Saturday 3

2005 SEPTEMBER Sunday 4

2005 SEPTEMBER Tuesday 6

A convoy of National Guard troops and supply trucks arrive with food and water for stranded people.

4,600
troops under the command of Lieutenant General Russel L. Honoré arrive to keep law and order.

The last people at the Superdome wait for buses. Thousands of people are still at the Convention Center.

Mayor Nagin tells people still in New Orleans to leave—the water is still too dangerous.

In 2000, about 485,000 people lived in the city of New Orleans.

New schools

Hurricane Katrina damaged more than 100 of the 128 schools in New Orleans. Thousands of children attended school in other states for the rest of the school year. People wanted to make the schools better once they were rebuilt.

2005 SEPTEMBER Wednesday 14

2005 SEPTEMBER Saturday 24

2006 JUNE

TODAY

$$

FEMA begins to set up mobile-home cities for hundreds of thousands of homeless people.

Hurricane Rita strikes just west of where Katrina had hit, causing more damage.

Workers start to remove 200,000 damaged cars from New Orleans.

Most of the levees and defenses in New Orleans have been rebuilt, in an eight-year project that cost $14.5 billion.

OVER SIZE LOAD

Today, only 369,000 do.

Stranded

The first attempts to repair the broken levees failed,

Find out more
about the final
evacuation on
pages 50–51.

Still waiting
Some people were
stranded for more than a
week. Many had to swim
to reach their rescuers
because it was too difficult
to get boats through
the debris.

so the waters continued to flood the city.

Destruction

Along 70 miles (113 km) of the Gulf Coast, strong winds and flooding ruined homes and lives.

In a whirl

Katrina's spinning winds created 62 tornadoes across 8 states.

Hurricane Katrina blasted across 90,000 square miles of land (233,000 sq km)

320 million large trees were killed or damaged

300,000 homes were destroyed

1,836 people died

1.5 million people left their homes

$75 billion was spent on emergency relief

62 tornadoes—
22 in Mississippi and Alabama alone

504 boats
were left on dry land

Across Mississippi, 49,950 utility poles had to be **repaired**

705 people **are still** listed as missing

7.4 million gallons of oil **poured into the water**

(28 million L)

200,000 vehicles were wrecked

52 oil platforms **were lost** and 58 damaged

operations.

Everybody out!

More than a million people left their homes along the Gulf Coast. They scattered across the United States, staying with relatives or in shelters, churches, or the homes of well-wishers.

Where did people go?

To Houston
Over 220,000 people went to Houston, TX. Many stayed in a health center set up in the Astrodome stadium.

To Baton Rouge
About 200,000 took a shorter journey to Baton Rouge, LA, almost doubling the city's population.

Mobile homes
FEMA set up 203,000 mobile homes and trailers to house those who had nowhere else.

The Red Cross's Safe and Well website helped people

Homeless

Alice Jackson lost her house and nearly all her possessions to the storm.

> 66 Before Katrina came through, I thought, 'If my house gets washed away, I'll just stay at my mother's house or my brother's house'— never thinking all our homes would be destroyed. . . . Everyone in my family is now a refugee. 99

—**Alice Jackson,
Ocean Springs, MS**

Seeking shelter

All along the Gulf Coast, people were desperate for shelter. Some camped in military-style tent cities or special storm shelters. Others slept in gyms, sports arenas, church basements, and volunteers' homes.

find one another.

Helping hands

Survivors no longer had homes or jobs. They needed help to get food, shelter, clothes, and health care. Tens of thousands of people from all over the United States volunteered to help.

Water and food
Food and clean drinking water were desperately needed. All the shops were shut or had been emptied of goods.

Clothes
People were left with only the clothes they were wearing. National appeals were made for donations.

First aid
These kits were vital, because there were very few doctors available.

A big job
Charities such as the Red Cross gave out emergency supplies and money.

Cleanup
Volunteers helped clean up debris, gut houses, and cut up fallen trees.

Building
Tools and materials were needed for repairing destroyed homes. Volunteer builders gave hundreds of thousands of hours of their time.

Music aid
Charities replaced thousands of instruments for musicians who had lost theirs.

Animal victims

Many animals had a tough time because of Katrina. But some pets have amazing survival stories.

#4892 D106
MISSING OWNER

04532   D-401
Owner Missing

D-222 No Home
3691 Owner Missing

Found at PMAC #D53
4456 Found but
"Sweetie" being Fostered
by B.R. resident

found D109   4899

Left behind

About 250,000 pets, from cats and dogs to birds and fish, were left behind in New Orleans. Sadly, very many of those left behind died.

Desperate owners pinned up pictures of their lost pets.

Stray dogs that had escaped from flooded houses roamed the streets.

Zoo success

The Audubon Zoo in New Orleans lost only 3 animals out of 1,400. It was on high ground, and the staff planned well.

44 percent of people who chose to stay and ride out the

> 66 When we first saw them, they were really starving. When they saw their trainers, they were absolutely flipping. 99

—Moby Solangi, president of Marine Life Oceanarium, Gulfport, MS

Dolphin joy

Eight dolphins were swept out of their aquarium. They were found out at sea, where their trainers kept them safe.

Carter with Cupcake, whom she had to leave behind when she fled ....

> 66 I lost a grandfather in the hurricane. To find a little kitty survived six months, that's great. . . . She is a gift, she is here to let us know there is hope. 99

—Tristan Carter, New Orleans

storm did so to care for their pets.

A new start

Katrina was the deadliest and most destructive hurricane to strike the United States in nearly 100 years. It cost lives and money, but many lessons have been learned.

The Superdome reopened in 2006.

Building a new life

1 New levees

An improved system of levees, floodwalls, and pumps aims to keep water out of New Orleans.

2 Better barriers

Workers are rebuilding barrier islands that have been lost during the last 100 years.

3 New houses

Organizations have helped build houses that will be able to cope with future large storms.

Katrina cost $108 billion in damage to property.

Blue roofs

One task was to keep rain out of buildings that had damaged roofs. Operation Blue Roof, run by the US Army Corps of Engineers, covered 81,000 roofs.

eye **EYEWITNESS**
Game on!

" We may have picked ourselves back up, . . . but we will never forget. And when [the New Orleans Saints] went to that Super Bowl in 2010, it was a big step toward a normal life for this city. It brought back a confidence and pride . . . that some of us had forgotten after the storm. "

—Teresia Schimmel,
New Orleans

······· the new Superdome

Kids' memories

66 The Saturday before the storm, . . . the Weather Channel, Fox News, and [a local news station] all told us that the now Category 5 storm, named Katrina, was headed straight for us. 99

—**Taylore Norton**

66 I was 17 years old. . . . Eventually the storm stopped and the water went down. . . . There was so much trash and debris all over the place. There was no electricity, no plumbing, no water. 99

—**Hannah Galloway**

66 I can remember, and will never forget, sitting on the bed of the Sleep Inn hotel in Baton Rouge, watching the numerous reports on Hurricane Katrina. . . . I was only 11 at the time. 99

—**Anonymous**

66 I was around the young age of 9 or 10 during Katrina. . . . I remember . . . every single hotel room in every bordering state was full. 99

—**Anonymous**

66 We packed some snacks, some clothes for three days, and my grandmother's large air tank. Everything else, we left behind. . . . My dad was boarding up our windows. . . . [He] is a fireman and had to stay behind. 99

—**Anonymous**

"I was very aware of what was going on. . . . [But] I didn't

66 I was just an 11-year-old boy from Chalmette, Louisiana, who, along with 15 other family members, evacuated to Baton Rouge to escape Hurricane Katrina. . . . When I did go back, I stood outside my house and just stared at it. . . . I cried to my mom all day. **99**

—Anonymous

66 Though I thought it couldn't get worse when the hurricane ruined my 17th birthday, the days after are hurting much more. **99**

—Craig Gilliam

66 The National Guard came and got us in two boats. . . . There were nine of us: my mother, father, and all my brothers and sisters. They didn't take us to the Superdome. They just dropped us off on the Causeway Bridge. We slept on the bridge for four days before we could get on the bus and come to Houston. . . . It was horrible. **99**

—Geranika Richardson

expect my life to be completely flipped upside down."

Glossary

barrier island
An island close to a shore that helps protect the shore from the sea.

breach
To break through or make a gap in something.

buoy
A floating marker that shows boats where to go or collects information.

canal
A human-made channel that carries water across land.

charity
An organization that raises money and provides help for people who are in trouble.

concrete
A hard, strong building material.

convoy
A group of people or vehicles that travel together.

curfew
A rule that orders people to stay indoors at certain times.

debris
The pieces of something that has been destroyed.

devastate
To damage seriously or destroy.

dropsonde
An instrument dropped from a plane into a storm in order to collect information.

evacuation
Removal from a dangerous area.

evacuee
A person who has left or been removed from a dangerous area.

eye
The calm, clear area at the center of a hurricane.

eye wall
The ring of storms around the eye of a hurricane.

hazard
Something dangerous.

hurricane
A violent storm with heavy rain and strong winds of at least 74 mph (119 kph).

inland
Away from the sea.

I-wall
A concrete wall that is planted into the ground to make a levee taller and prevent flooding.

landfall
The point at which a hurricane's eye crosses land after forming over water.

levee
A high earth wall next to a river or lake, built to keep the area around it from flooding.

mandatory
Ordered by a rule or law.

National Guard
A volunteer military organization with units in each state.

relief
Help given to people in trouble.

Saffir-Simpson scale
A series of ratings that describe how strong a hurricane is, based on how fast its winds are. The scale goes from Category 1 to Category 5.

satellite
A spacecraft that travels around Earth and collects scientific information or transmits messages.

storm surge
A rise in sea level caused by a storm.

stranded
Left in a strange or unpleasant place.

tornado
A violent, twisting windstorm in the shape of a funnel.

tropical storm
A storm that forms over warm waters and has winds of 39–73 mph (63–118 kph). A tropical storm can become a hurricane if its winds get faster.

wetlands
Areas of low, damp land. Swamps and marshes are wetlands.

Index

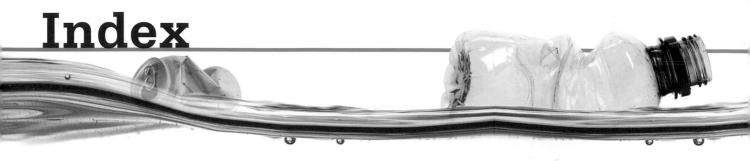

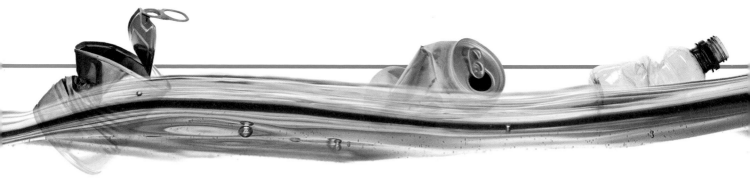

Thank you

Alamy Images: 12 plane bg, 13 plane bg (Flight Plan), 13 br (PFMIX); AP Images: 56 br (Bill Haber), 33 c (Brett Coomer/*Houston Chronicle*), 20, 21, 54 bl (Cheryl Gerber), 26 bl, 33cr, 54 c bg, 55 c bg (Dave Martin), 32 cl, 32 cr, 33 t (David J. Phillip), 54 br (Don Ryan), 22, 23, 32 c (Eric Gay), 54 tl photos (Haraz N. Ghanbari), 3 br, 55 br (John Amis), cover bl, 25 br (John Bazemore), 26 br (Mari Darr-Welch), 45 bc (Melissa Phillip/*Houston Chronicle*), 34 b bg, 35 b (Paul Saneya), 44 bcr (Robert Galbraith), 55 t (Steve Helber), 19 c (Tom Worner/*Tyler Morning Telegraph*), 25 bl, 26 tr, 27 tl, 30, 31, 36 bl bg, 40 bc, 46, 47 (Vincent Laforet), 1 (Vincent Laforet/*The New York Times*), 38 tr (William Colgin/*Mississippi Press-Register*); Corbis Images/Reuters: 12 tl (Molly Riley), 27 bl (Robert Galbraith); Dreamstime: cover bg t waves, back cover bg t waves (Emevil), cover bg b waves, back cover bg b waves (Fotolotti), back cover bl (Manaemedia), 52 water bottles (Zls); EPA.gov: 24 cl; FEMA: 50 bl (Andrea Booher), 50 bc (Ed Edahl), 56 bl (Jacinta Quesada), 50 cr (Jennifer Smits), 27 cr (Jocelyn Augustino), 57 t (John Fleck), 50 br (Marilee Caliendo), 33 cl (Marty Bahamonde), 39 cr (Patricia Brach), 44 br, 45 bl (Sharon Karr), 38 tl (Win Henderson), 35 cl; Fotolia: 56 t, 57 t bg (Ed Metz), 15 bl (Temistocle Lucare); Getty Images: 16 t bg, 17 t bg (Calvin Gavlon Jr.), 51 b (Joe Raedle), 18 cr (JupiterImages), 34 b, 42, 43, 50 t, 51 t bg (Mario Tama); iStockphoto: 5 t fg l (314), 8 cl, 36 tr frame, 45 c (4x6), 29 chickens (adipelcz), 18 can (AdrianHancu), 53 broom and bin (alacatr), 53 r crate (amriphoto), 32 t bg, 33 t bg (Andrea Preibisch), 52 boots (AndreasReh), 53 boards (AndrewJohnson), 9 br photo (Aneese), 9 cl, 24 cr (arcady_31), 54 tr (Astakhova), 2 tr, 34 t (BanksPhotos), 37 br (Bigandt_Photography), 14 bl (BlackJack3D), 36 bl frame (blackred), 17 crb (Bluefont), 37 tr frame, 37 cr frame (bphillips), 44 cr (Brilt), 60 bg, 61 bg (ceth), 25 t (cpurser), back cover tl (DanCardiff), 41 bl (dlewis33), 15 bcl, 44 bl (DNY59), 52 b clothing (DonNichols), 32 bl, 33 bottle, 62 tr, 63 tr (Dori OConnell), 19 br (Elhenyo), 44 cl (evirgen), 57 bl (FiledIMAGE), 44 c bg, 45 c bg (George Clerk), 48 tl trees (gepard001), 53 tr (gmattrichard), 37 cr (gmutlu), 40 bl (gradts), 9 cr (greyj), 14 cr (Grzegorz Petrykowski), 18 phone (hillaryfox), 53 sax (horiyan), 19 bl money (imagestock), 63 tl (iSebastian), 53 tools (ivanastar), 48 br money bags (jehsomwang), 8 cr (jfmdesign), 52 t box (JoeLena), 52 Band-Aid (joxxxxjo), 2 b bg, 3 b bg, 24 b bg, 25 b bg (Jynne), 52 aid kit (lcs813), 52 cans (le_cyclope), 44 c, 49 cl ship (Leontura), 48 bl people (leremy), 54 c (LindaMarieB), 16 b water, 17 b water (lubilub), 44 b road, 45 b road (Maksymowicz), 18 radio (mgkaya), 36 tl frame, 36 br frame, 37 bl frame (mict), 52 br box (miflippo), 2 t bg, 3 t bg, 24 t bg, 25 t bg (MihailUlianikov), 32 b, 33 b, 62 b, 63 b (monap), 32 waves, 33 waves, 62 waves, 63 waves (msheldrake), 9 t (narloch-liberra), 14 br (narvikk), 18 bg paper, 19 bg paper, 52 bg, 53 bg (Nastco), 12 bl (NikoNomad),

18 flashlight (Panya7), 4 t bg, 5 t bg (ParkerDeen), 14 bc (Patrick Heagney), 4 t fg, 9 bl, 61 br (Pgiam), 52 food box (photka), 26 concrete edge, 27 concrete edge (Photobvious), 45 cr (princessdlaf), 53 l crate (rbozuk), 37 tr (rmarnold), 37 tl frame, 37 br frame (robynmac), 4 b (schfer), 41 tr (SilviaJansen), 45 t (skynesher), 62 tl, 63 tc (snyferok), 36 tr (sooksunsaksit), 18 bg board, 19 bg board (sorendls), 52 crate (Talaj), 9 br cars (taoty), 24 bl (tomasworks), 53 contrabass (Valeriy Lebedev), 18 peas (VvoeVale), 15 bcr (Warren Price Photography), cover br (Whirler), 18 batteries (winterling), 18 Band-Aids (xactive), 52 t clothing (yellowsarah); Landov/Kathy Anderson/*The Times-Picayune*: 36 bl fg; Louisiana State Museum/Mark J. Sindler: 36 tl fg; NASA: 10 bg, 11 (GOES 12 Satellite, NOAA), 14 t bg, 15 t bg (Norman Kuring), 8 t; Courtesy of the New Orleans Fire Department: 35 cr; NOAA: 38 tc, 39 tl, 44 t (Lieut. Commander Mark Moran, NOAA Corps, NMAO/AOC), 13 tr (Paul Leighton), 38 bg, 39 bg (Wayne and Nancy Weikel, FEMA Fisheries Coordinators), cover tl, 6, 8 b bg, 12 tr, 13 bl; Redux/Vincent Laforet/*The New York Times*: 40 bg, 41 bg; Science Source: 12 br (Gregory Ochocki), 53 tl (Jim West), 56 bc (Julie Dermansky), 12 bc; Shutterstock, Inc.: 57 br (Action Sports Photography), 49 tornadoes (Alhovik), 19 bl keys (Arvind Balaraman), 45 cl (Atlaspix), 35 t (Baldas1950), 29 hydrant (Bill Fehr), 2 br, 24 bc (Brisbane), 17 tr (burnel1), 41 br (Eric Isselee), 16 cl (Faiz Zaki), 12 weather bg, 13 weather bg (Fer Gregory), 26 concrete cracks, 27 concrete cracks (fluke samed), 24 t (forestpath), 19 t (Galina Gutarin), 48 c trees (hackerkuper), 45 br (Huguette Roe), 10 t (lafoto), 36 bg, 37 bg (lemony), 14 cl (mezzotint), 17 br (Monkey Business Images), cover t bg, back cover t bg (Ollyy), 16 bl (Paul Robinson), 17 crt (Skalapendra), 16 cl grass (Smileus), 24 c bg, 25 c bg (Vaclav Volrab), 40 br (wannapong), 16 cr, 17 cl (YurkaImmortal); *The Shreveport Times*/Jessica Leigh: cover main, 36 br; Thinkstock: 8 bl screen (Believe_In_Me), 25 c clock (Dimedrol68), 8 c bg, 9 c bg (muratart), 15 br (nick shepherd), 25 person icon (Nixken), 5 t fg r, 51 t (Pattie Steib), 14 t (Vladimir Krivsun), 41 cr (zak00); US Air Force/Capt. Kevin Hynes: 64; US Navy: 35 c; US Coast Guard: 37 tl.

Special thanks to Francie Alexander, Rande Bynum, Phyllis C. Hunter, Suzanne McCabe, and Geranika Richardson.